THE BLINDMAN GO

The Blindman Goes From A To B

MAUREEN WILKINSON

PETERLOO POETS

First published in 1990
by Peterloo Poets
2 Kelly Gardens, Calstock, Cornwall PL18 9SA, U.K.

© 1990 by Maureen Wilkinson

All rights reserved. No part of this publication may be reproduced, stored in a retrieval system, or transmitted, in any form or by any means, electronic, mechanical, photocopying, recording or otherwise without the prior permission in writing of the publisher.

British Library Cataloguing in Publication Data
Wilkinson, Maureen
    The blindman goes from A to B.
    I. Title
821.914

ISBN 1-871471-15-X

Printed in Great Britain by
Latimer Trend & Company Ltd, Plymouth

ACKNOWLEDGEMENTS are due to the editors of *The Guardian, Poetry Matters, Poetry Review,* and *Westwords,* in whose pages some of these poems first appeared.

'Bringing the Night Cow Down' won 1st prize in the 1987 *Peterloo Poets Open Poetry Competition* and 'The Amnesiac's Dream' won 1st prize in the same competition in 1990.

'Only This' won a 4th prize in the 1988 *National Poetry Competition* and 'Pity the Dumb' won a £50 prize in the 1989 *National Poetry Competition.*

Seven of these poems were published in *Peterloo Preview 1* (Peterloo Poets, 1988).

Cover illustration: linocut by Maureen Wilkinson

Contents

page
- 9 Only This
- 10 Pity the Dumb
- 12 Sandra, I Have Your Photo Still
- 14 Hair
- 16 Bringing the Night Cow Down
- 18 The Inseminator's Tale
- 19 Dying; a Drama in Two Parts
- 20 This Poem is Walking its Dog
- 22 How to Paint Nature
- 24 Sisyphus
- 26 Steps
- 28 Plums
- 29 Beyond Silence
- 30 Spinning Straw to Gold
- 33 Every Tide
- 34 Pendulums
- 35 The Amnesiac's Dream
- 36 Portraits of a Fox
- 38 The Blindman Goes From A To B
- 40 Wishing for Tigers
- 42 Travellers' Tales
- 44 Dance Performance, Bali
- 45 Running
- 46 Yard
- 48 The Crime
- 50 Shit Heap
- 52 New Shoes
- 54 Memories are Mostly Made of This
- 55 Lessons in Ecstasy
- 58 Earth
- 60 Seeing Yellow
- 61 *Author's note*

Only This

The grief is so close to the joy that it flickers and flickers and flickers until we are blind with it.

Only a seaside town, an afternoon
of golden weather like a state of grace.
Above the sky hub where three roads converge
some wheeling pigeons spin a hollow drum
of tin-bright flight. People along the pier
sit basking, that their flesh may self-forget
itself in pleasure; briefly they become
ocean, pavement, distance, shadow, child.
An infant in a pram opens his eyes.
He invents sky. He ripens like a loaf.

Pity The Dumb

We didn't talk about him going blind.
Our Mother said it wasn't nice to question
just what he couldn't see, what *else* it changed.

Our Mother said we shouldn't tell our friends
or teachers, since we didn't want their pity.
At school we were as diligent and silent
as girls were meant to be. In private I
walked round with my eyes shut, to learn the facts.

At weekends he and I worked in the garden.
It was his larger cage. I mapped out space
with grids of sticks and string, and helped him pace
the scope of it. I fetched him picks and spades
to break the darkness, was his flat earth judge.
I drew him furrows. He spilled shining beans
into my hands. I kept
the burden of their beauty to myself,
and buried them precisely, line by line.
And at each summer's end we harvested.
I set his fork eight inches from each green
potato clump. He always kept
a silent stand, his eyes fixed on the sky,
while I sieved earth, gathered the fruits of light.

Our Mother said that many were worse off.
We had our food, a roof. Our mute restraint
became the straight and narrow she called fate.
She hung God's comforts up on china plates.
We kept our visions under house arrest.

Our lives grew coiled inwards, like a shell.
I learnt the landscape of his bell-jar dark.
Learnt how the shut self shrinks, until its voice
is no more than a stone dropped in a shaft
of water, with the thin
concentric circles spreading in a grief,
of echoes you can't catch and cannot touch.

Till all the dreamed of selves edge out of sight.

Sandra, I Have Your Photo Still

You spent your childhood in and out of care.
This snap was taken on a council trip
to Broadstairs by a social worker whose
name you'd long forgotten. She perhaps
had called you, for it seems you're smiling back,
from your sand-castles.
A small girl of six.

It was the only image of yourself
you had retained from all your fifteen years.
I still recall your half embarrassed crack
about not having changed,
although in fact
you'd grown up inches taller than I was,
and Snoopy T shirts couldn't hide your breasts.

I still remember teaching you to read.
How you were shy to speak the childish text,
and how you liked to barricade your desk
with books and chairs, and how meticulously
you'd paste blue paper in your locker space,
to keep your things inside its tiny cell.

Some people seem to get themselves misplaced
at birth. You surely warranted a better fate
than shiftless parents and their part-time love.

I still remember how you used to swear
at my insistence you do this or that.
Your 'Fuck offs,' uttered with the sweetest smiles
assumed a comic grace. You'd bring
the school's grey rabbit into class
for comfort, as you finished off your work.

You brought the photo in on my last day.
By now you must be twenty five or six.
I keep it as a talisman, which
by virtue of its fragile thread of love
might keep you from those legacies of loss,
which hand on past misfortunes like a curse.

I hope somebody loves you, that by now
you've got a home and children of your own.
Perhaps you'll see within an offspring's face
a likeness which assimilates your own
lost childhood image, which I'm keeping safe.
Sandra, I have your photo still.

Hair

Aged two, I overheard an aunt remark
it curious that we should look alike
though my hair was so blonde, and yours so dark.
I'd only thought you older, until then.

This insight prompted me scrutinize
our cut-off colours drifting to the floor,
when we sat mirror-trapped on swivel chairs,
in that barbaric shop in Peckham Rye.
Afterwards I often stooped to collect
our magic fragments back. I'd hide them home
curled in my separate hands like secret birds.

Till you were seven we both wore the same
Centre-parted bobs with ribbon bows
on top like silken ears. About that time
I chanced to have a grim prophetic dream
in which we were both adults and both wore
our long hair hanging loose, yours dark, mine light,
the way that we had grown it when you died.
But sticking to the facts;

our school-days passed ummemorably coiffured as
short or plaits. We seem to grow into allotted roles
like star-struck sisters from a fairy tale.
Perhaps the sobriety of your dark brows
gave you your air of rational good sense,
while I had only insubstantial light
like gossamer above a weighted seed.

As teenagers we both flirted with fashion,
and practiced flick-ups, bouffants and the like.
You soon cast off these trivial pursuits
to join the Red Cross. I discovered sex.

Later as students we both grew our hair.
You started nursing and I studied Art.
You pinned your long hair up in a sleek bun.
I left mine hanging loose. I married young
and had two babies during my degree,
while you went on to pass midwifery.

You died in an air crash at twenty-four.
Our distraught Mother, clearing out your things
piled in my arms your clothes, your shoes, your books,
your half-made knitting which she couldn't bear
to keep or finish.

But somehow didn't see you'd left behind
a plastic hair brush strung with your dark hairs,
pliant and strong, and shining as in life,
still perfumed with the lacquer that you wore.

Bringing the Night Cow Down

Beyond the door a sea of plunging dark,
a blinding overlay of turbulence,
a star-struck forest-crush of broken airs, a
leafy-lashing fingering of wet
which I now measure, fathom, piece and part
to milk the cow,
to bring the night cow down.

That swell of bovine yellow, sodden dark, too
silage sweet, too bruised with sweeping night
to find in fields. So come
my wallow one,
my grazing manatee, fill out your hide
with wind, with leather wings,
the moon has drowned, the sun's extinguished, all
the daisy stars
have floated off much higher than our sight
and undulate in phosphorescent tides. Come lumbering plush
below the milky way,
though winds lock milk-wet fingers in our path
answer my cry
and bring the night cow down.

What lack of rhyme or reason guides this task, repeated nightly?
Brightly, from this hill
my house stands firmly anchored;
tele's on,
electric light has tamed the sucked up air,
the books have formed a regiment of words,
the walls are vertical, the carpet's square,
the roof's a sanity of tessellation.
The needling rain tattoos my docile flesh, and spreads in coloured
 cold
like peacocks' eyes.
No longer seeing, I reach in the dark
a denser shadowing, a brew of grass, a swaying cauldron-hide,
and the opacity of her black breath.

Come
steaming bulk. We're turning to the light. I hear your sway
descend the clumping path, the flattened lumping rushes of the
 hill.
Come coloured cow, the Chagall of my heart
and manifest your density of light.
Come, let me milk the whiteness of the dark.

The Inseminator's Tale

Who is this stranger, wearing fancy dress?
A surgeon's smock, high boots, one
filmy glove. He flicks the square lid from his silver flask.
White vapours are exhaled, and they drift,
around the frozen capsules, stained dark blue.

The cow's brought in and tied. She sighs and shuffles
to register her boredom and annoyance.

He edges up behind her, eyes alert.
Across his mouth quivers a silver cane, like
a flamenco dancer's rose. There is no point
in talking to one with lips thus engaged.
I entertain the cow with murmurings.
His gloved arm slips up her anatomy. 'She's right on,' he
affirms congenially.
His sterile cupid's arrow finds its mark.

I free the cow. I wonder if she misses
courtship, even sexual satisfaction. The lumbering bull,
with all his sniff and savour,
his mooning eyes and lusty consummations,
has been replaced in her annals of romance,
by one discarded gauntlet, somewhat stained.

And
does she feel a sense of being changed,
as Silver Patrick's semen (Charolais),
swiftly defrosts. This is her sixth conception.
While poor duped Silver Patrick, never knowing
where all his seed so lightly spilled is going,
continues in his joyless copulations,
with half a cow skin on a wooden frame.

Dying; a Drama in Two Parts

Hen's head, alert, alarmed,
attempts to will
her feathery slack to plump again with breath.
Amnesic now, her broken flute of bones
cannot remember their small repertoire.

She clearly is a goner.
As I lift
the unstrung marionette of her poor flesh,
she elevates her shrewd reptilian gaze.
I watch her watching me put her to death.

My feet are on the pole across her neck.
The first pull leaves her stirring; me in doubt.
I try again, detaching her flame head,
which falls with folded eyes,
a scarlet flower.

Her broken carcass starts to strut about.

This Poem is Walking its Dog

This poem is walking its dog
along an undulating lane.
The views are blinkered by dry stone hedges.
Only from hilltops, and at farm gateways
do the orderly vistas open.
The distant sea tops the land like a conjuring trick.
This is a dull walk, all things considered.
If a painting were walking its dog, and not a poem
it would be possible to replicate this scene
with a palette containing only
black, white, prussian blue and yellow.
The autumnal bracken is assuming
the colour and aspect of flame,
and the poem is tempted to sidetrack along a turn of phrase,
but the dog introduces objectivity by pulling hard
ahead between the green banks burning, and the poem begins to
    read
the wayside notices, which are all painted on scraps of white
formica; CREAM TEAS, BED AND BREAKFAST, FRESH
    FARM EGGS, GOAT
PRODUCTS, CAMPING, COWS CROSSING, CREAM BY
    POST.
The acceleration of the dog and the poem
startles a flock of rooks, which swim the air in a double helix.
The birds had been roosting in a group of sycamore trees,
which are already losing their leaves.
The trees are in army camouflage.
Their silhouette is like ash pushed by a finger on a white formica
    table.
In a field to the left is a beautiful golden pyramid
of spiralling big-baled straw. It is built up from a base of
twelve. 12,9,6,2. The farmer must have been short of
the final bale. Clover leaves are sticking to the poem's
wellington boots like mandalas in triptych, and the combination
    seems
somehow significant, so that a philosophic quote in Greek
would be nice, a la Ezra Pound, but

unfortunately both the dog and the poem
are ignorant in these matters.
Now they are adjacent to the reservoir
which neatly curtails the collective valleys of six hills. The water
lies flat like a jigsaw piece of the sky.
The dog is engrossed in his own observations which
he may or may not later compile into a poem. His medium
is the secret and esoteric world of
scents and aromas. He is building a model of the present
upon the history of the recent past, and from this he will
   postulate
the future. The clouds have formed themselves into a giant V like
a Blake painting, or the finger of God. In the village
they turn for home. Here, as ever
a bay and white horse is standing in a field which is next to
a bay and white rocking-horse in a council house garden.
The rocking-horse is frozen in an attitude of perpetual motion,
rather like the poem,
but the dog is intent on movement.
He is utterly absorbed in the phenomenon of himself THE DOG
   moving
as if he had assimilated some of Gurdieff's writings on
self-wakefulness. They are walking along the instruction 'SLOW'
painted on the road at a tight bend.
The dog is panting. He is a red dog.
He is the colour of bracken burning between the green hedges.
A cabbage-white butterfly is crossing the stile of a public
   footpath.
Now they are home, and since the dog and the poem and the
   walk are
leashed together,
they reach the front door in perfect unison.

How to Paint Nature

(from the title of an instructional book)

First make yourself a suitable view-finder
out of stiff card, it may be square or oblong.
Then using this device select a fragment
whose attributes of colour, line and content
enhance your decor and your reputation.

Beware! Remain objective and alert.
It's sometimes felt that thinking man himself
is but a warp in Nature's massive weft.

People insist that certain subjects choose them;
thorn hedges etched against a milky sky,
a cleverly dovetailed set of hills,
bludgeoning flowers (beware of local colour),
all come to mind, along with autumn woodlands,
and seascapes, captured with the sun half set.

So now, equipped with brushes, board and pigment
(page six advises on the basic kit),
prepare to catch her!
She's kaleidoscopic,
employing endless multi-level shifts.

A word about abstraction; in the sense
of *bringing out* some single quality
such as pure cubic form, you may well find
that such techniques can ease the course of Art.
Likewise *impressionism*. Let's be frank.
There's no way that your fragile mix and match
can ever emulate reality.

Don't let your hobby gain the upper hand.
Like Nature, Art's inclined to anarchy.
Like Nature, Art is wasteful, cruel, mundane,
erotic, sacred and tyrannical, and
also magic: holding unseen mirrors to
unseen puzzles, un-
imaginable solutions,
reveal themselves and travel off at tangents.
Better to make your copies, sane and straight
(if second rate), than pursue these deflections.

We hope that you get pleasure from your pictures
of Nature plagiarized, plus frame and hook, but
making Art which plagiarizes Nature
is not within the functions of this book.

Sisyphus

Work,
by Bertram Russell's definition,
is moving matter within space and time.
So Sisyphus' task with hill and stone
was qualitively really much the same as
roles most mortals adopt willingly. Work's
more of a *commitment* than a *curse*; (that's
given the pragmatics of compulsion.)

How often have we all read in the news
about some lucky sod who's free to choose
to let his stone roll back and gather moss. It's
'BUS CONDUCTOR SCOOPS A MASSIVE WIN.'
He's got eight draws up on the Vernon's Pools.
A photo shows him smiling with his wife.
The caption quotes him, 'Money won't change *my* life.
We don't plan moving
and I'll keep my job,
(although the missus thinks she'll go part-time.)
We all know nowadays work don't grow on trees.
Work's pensionable! Work lends dignity!
I've asked around my mates, and they agree.'
(Like Sisyphus his cry is 'On top please!')
So while we're chatting,
could you pass the stone.

We women are past-masters at the art
of uphill struggles. Conditioned or cursed
by upbringings and brain-wash magazines,
necessities, and fragile self-esteem, we
keep balls rolling,
keep the damn house clean,
fill kids with food, put
clothes in the machine, and
that's before we start on our careers.
Our ideal jobs aren't the stone rolling kind.
A luscious body *and* a lively mind's

the least we're after. (Just pass us the stones.)
We shop at lunch-times, keep on rolling then
our figures won't grow bigger than size ten.
Mythologies cite warnings from the past:
stop trying girls, and you'll go downhill fast.
It's up to you make the loving last!
Sisyphus raised one stone; we raise more.
Their rumblings keep the wild wolves from the door.
With effort we appease the angry gods,
who doubtlessly are keeping their own score,
equating excellence with each ascent.
Each day reveals more stones, more slopes, more peaks.
It seems so normal that we're scared to stop.
Though time falls darkly as an obelisk.

Shared toil fosters camaraderie.
Our stoic protests, uttered half in jest
ring through the lonely valleys we can't bridge. It's:
'*donkeys go best loaded, don't you know.*
There's no rest for the wicked. It's all go.
Good life if you don't weaken. Stitch in time.
The devil will find work for idle hands.'

Meantime,
the devil's sitting on his stone
amidst the beauty of the hills and skies.
Thoughts of eternity light up his eyes.

The idle always did show enterprise.

Steps

As breath, each step flies from its compressed shadow
to haul her higher. Now she's near the top
and pauses in the rain. She's counting back
a waterfall of ledges, like a fan
to see how far she's climbed. The granite slabs
had inverted her image, held her drowning,
but now she stands quiescent, and her ghosts
float down as oil on water. She observes
the High Street like a stage set, simple, flat
with distant figures moving left or right.
She's carrying a bag of groceries
which pulls one shoulder low, keeps one arm stretched.
She doesn't set it down, but lets her gaze
rest on the sky's white emptiness, which frays
into oblique bright rain, as if a blade
had slashed repeatedly across the grey

townscape. If this image was a photograph
materialising in a dark-room tray,
it could be lifted, dripping, to the light.
Then she would see herself reflected against the flat
paper hillside, against the long stairway,
and nothing would move except, in the reflection,
the linear fingers of raindrops
etching her face.

It would be a simple step
to roll up the scene like a paper lantern
so that the rain opened into light
and the granite stairs joined, end to beginning, in a circle
with a woman forever pausing, looking back
or else, a moment earlier, or a moment later, forever caught
in climbing the shadow wheel,
and cogged time held like breath.

She does not think of this. She simply rests, letting
herself mirror the paper sky.
She is a white absence; a cut out scrap-book woman
whose likeness is kept elsewhere.

And now she turns to climb the final slabs.
As breath, each step flies from its compressed shadow,
and at the top she's high enough to see
the harbour, and an opaque arc of sea
pock-marked with liquid eyes.

Except she doesn't turn. The channelled sky
above her is an arrow, pointing down.

Plums

These are the first Victoria plums of the Autumn.
An old lady has just bought some to share with her friend.

Just a bag of plums, nothing else.

Now they are standing outside the big open-fronted greengrocer's
   shop
and each has a purple plum in her hand.
One old lady is also holding the brown paper bag.
They cannot wait to taste the new fruit but
they are too old to be able to eat and walk
at the same time. Each one pushes a plum into her mouth.
The juice runs, purple and gold.
They do not speak, although they make little noises
of appreciation to each other. They each take a second plum but
they do not risk eating and walking at the same time.
The plum stones are dropped decorously back into the bag.
There are still a few plums left.
They move on cautiously,
as if the pavement might grow chasms.

Beyond Silence

At dawn the moth-beats of your sleeping breath
fashion a mantle in the pin-point dark.

All day I have been listening for a sound beyond silence.

I am accustomed to the inwardness of granite,
and my land-lakes, green in their hammocks
make little enough sound.

Even the air today would seem to comply
to the general theme.
It is not lively, blowing in flames,
but is alabaster, rising
to unsheath its box-file of scenery
item by item.

Yet ever bursting on the emptiness,
something beyond hearing oscillates,
is inchoate with syllables which thunder.

Where then is the vanishing point,
the pure out-of-sight?

This image comes to mind as if from a long way off:
my own solitary figure, and this scythed hill
under the sickle sky.

I see it like an enormous shout.

Spinning Straw to Gold

Between day's clarity, and night's small death,

> *She had three attributes;*
> *beauty, filial love, a gift for spinning.*

an open truck arrives, loaded with straw.

> *Her Father, predestined to reckless pride,*
> *boasted that she could spin straw to gold.*

I stack the bales in a block of light,
while in the barn my placid, brindled calves
press cloven hooves into their bed of dung.
And as I work the poem makes itself;
a party game of word associations.
Events, like beads, slipped on the spun-out yarn.

Yet if the calves knew words they would not have
language for winter, since this is their first.
They only would speak grass, and milk and . . .

> *Maier, alchemist, thought gold was spun*
> *around the earth by orbits of the sun.*

They'd have no word for straw, which might be gold,
stacked up in fat, bright ingots.

> *The King heard rumours of the golden girl*
> *and hatched a scheme to test her purity.*

Bedding the cattle down with two split bales.
I sow straw-yellow onto the dung-brown.
The bullocks, fat brown trout, bridle and dart
dragging the pigment in their ponderous dance.
The floor is filled, four corners, the whole square
with yellow, hard-edged as a Mondrian.

> *The King locked the girl in a room of straw*
> *with just her spinning wheel for company.*
> *If she succeeded she would be his bride.*
> *She twisted wheaten blades into a rope.*
> *She knew that if she failed she would die.*

The cows and I are moving through a fable;
handwritten, in illuminated text.

> *The stars arranged themselves in constellations*
> *of pure disinterest. She slept on the straw,*
> *and in the morning found it spun to gold.*

> *An elfin man appeared like Lucifer.*
> *He told her that the price of her salvation,*
> *of straw's trancendence, was her first-born child.*
> *It seemed she spun a vacillating thread*
> *of dross to gold to dross to gold*
> *to dross.*

Now I'm outside, a shadow within shade,
comprised of separate densities of darkness.
Reality appears to alternate
between a seamless web, and isolation.
The flying bobbin of its alternation
weaving a trailing shadow, much like grief.

> *By chance the girl, now Queen, found out the spell
> which was the elfin's name. She spoke the word
> and got to keep the lot: King, gold and child.*

Gold is not transmutable, and straw
breaks down to earth, which then grows straw again.
Also it is hollow. Thus the trickster,
adding his fable to the poem's spin,
naively brought his people into danger
then, through a straw, he led them out again.

I stand alone, a shadow in the dark.

> *She slept alone, a shadow in the dark.*

We clutch at straws, to let the gold flood in.

Every Tide

Her kitchen window faced onto the sea;
the sea her echo, and her company.
She spent each morning at her laundry,
dipping and wringing, though her flying hands
grew older, older as her linens drowned.

She worked for absolution. Every tide
returned with its fresh burdens.
Waters soared. All was submerged, replenished,
rinsed and drained.
She met the crested rivers, blue and white.
The pattern of her days swam by like moons.

Wearily the ocean watched, and wept,
as music grieves upon its rooted thread.
Its task was also feminine: to grind,
refining every shore and stone to sand,
remaking matter into running time.
Rocks into pebbles. Everything made smooth.

Then on her little land, cut from the hill,
she strung the beating sheets, as white as wings.
Air was her witness, and her medium.
She saw the sun was fastened to the stars,
day on, day on and all things in accord.
The ocean sang and grieved against its bed.

Pendulums

After we had double-hemmed the sand's perimeter
we sat for a while outside the cliff-top cafe
in order to watch the sea's respiration
on the shore. All around us people were drinking tea
or waiting for teas to be served.
On the beach below a small boy
was running continuously back and forth with the ocean's
   pendulum.
Into the edge of each receding wave he was pouring
a spadeful of dry sand.

At three o'clock the tide began to turn.

Meantime, as orders became ready in the kitchen
the cafe owner shouted out their numbers.
'Eighty-nine.' 'Ninety.'
'Ninety-one.' 'Ninety-two.'
A moment later, 'Ninety-three.'

The Amnesiac's Dream

It seems my face is now a race of clouds:
some of them dragons, some of them galleons,
or birds, or ghosts of words, or brief charades.
You must excuse me shouting, but my mouth's
a dome of wind. I really don't know who
sent all these dreams, the one about a bowl
of yellow sand, the one about a grave
shaped like a woman's body made of sky.
The one about the edge that shapes away
into a blindman's template, and you have
to guess its continent. I keep consulting
oracles: I've been the Empress, the Moon
and the Hanged Man. I have been swords
crossed in a corn field. I've loosed flocks of birds
from my raised hands. They sky-write in a swarm
of rapid hieroglyphics which reveal
my name, my future, everything, except
I can't decipher it quite fast enough
to keep pace with the tempo of their wings
erasing air's white pages, which contain
the poem of myself, which I forgot.

At the same time it seems I am a void
in which impressions darken without trace,
while secretly inside me they remake
this landscape, like the network of a brain
without a wiring diagram. It seems
I am a crazy bank of films
with different plots, but playing all at once;
a shadow play, a child's construction kit
made up with some improbable mistakes.
It seems I am decked out in all my loves. My fingerprints are made
of your warm skin, and time is scars and banners, and it seems
my bones are bedrock granite sunk so deep
they cannot speak, though they know everything.
It seems as if my throat's an unknown song.
It seems the tides are levied by my breath.
It seems that I might drown in memory.

Portraits of a Fox

The first fox I ever saw was in my garden.
I was young, and could not sleep,
but stood in the dark at an upstairs window
in my honey-comb house.

Chalk steps cut into the woodland hill
held rows of terraced houses, bricked together
as red and resolute as lego. The estate
so new that our unfenced gardens joined
in a milky trough

of chalk, which was the crush of sea-shells spent
and subdued as snow as they heaped
in hills of death. Sometimes I dreamed
that phantom seas still breathed
through the valley's crucible,

though in reality the roof-tops queued
their rows of triangles like rigid waves,
sky-skin of blades which did not sway or break,
though my anchored children slept
in their chrysalid beds.

Then the lone fox came as a gift against old bones.

Later I made a portrait of this first
fox I had ever seen.
In fact I painted it as many foxes,
and made them flames to knit the broken dark.
To fathom the sweet darks of that flayed land
and be my emissaries.

Since then I have seen foxes many times, and
even tonight, as I walked along
the labyrinthine lanes and
in through the gate where the fields fall down
to thicken in the valley's groin.

Fox and fox-watcher move as motives etched
along a Möbius strip,
the distance twisting closed
until they meet.

Slow amber moving through the mute of dusk,
fox paused. I saw the instant of its eyes
mirror my zeroed likeness. Then time turned:
fox turned upon the instant of touched time
to melt my after-image in the dark.

The Blindman Goes From A To B

My somewhere hands divine absence.
Edge extends as a ley-line,
grows itself by hand-spans into a wall,
which is my half-crutch, and my rolling rail.

Thus I row along.
Night-fly, fast as a roving eye,
with my someplace feet keeping me informed
of their extra-sensory perceptions.
I shuffle on the good-time path, flat as water shine.

I have mortified the strength of my thighs:
still my steps make nimble time.
I tread narrow, narrow as a circus horse, keeping
to the tight-rope twist of correct oblivion, until
my hand-prop shapes away.

Now I am womb-blind, resting on a sky which
cradles me. My mind's eye, finger's mind, spine's heart
make rapid re-assessments. At every boundary,
at the skin's press,
darkness barters with darkness.

This is where space yawns into a sideways.
Leaves milk my hand, their skins as light as
dancing girls. Sky makes a lagoon, with
the big air-animals stooping to drink.
I can hear the trees reading aloud
from the braille of the clouds. The text contains
both jokes and melancholy passages.
Branches have switched on their carousels.
They sing in rounds, their wooden horses riding.

Edge! My feet have put on their fear-brakes.
Something slams by, heavy as cut.
It abducts a vacuum, into which the dead airs
bury themselves. My senses grow cilia, reaching out
for any suddenness, although roads are a limited danger zone;
twelve paces, or twenty. I count across. Now, nearing home,
I recite the edges by heart:
a clipped hedge, sorrowing.
My fingers comfort its bereavement.
Thirty-seven noble railings.
Here my garden curls to greet me, its perfumes
surfing on the wind. The path wears worry lines
so as not to show its love.
My mid-season roses have auras in three colours.
My key completes the eye of the lock.

Wishing for Tigers

Even at night the jungle is not silent.
Its effervescent energy reminds me
of white noise on a television screen;
a sense of bright coherence, beyond sight,
which culminates in a fragmented scream.

Our guide book says the last six Java tigers
once lived within this forty square mile patch.
They're thought to be extinct, though recently
a study group found one huge feline paw-print
pressed into mud along a river bank.

No one else is staying at the lodge.
She brings us coffee. We don't speak her language
but smile to thank her. Mime to show the weather
delays our leaving. Sheets of opaque rain
slam down from the veranda. We can just
make out her garden, her small moon of grass.

She sees my camera and indicates
she'd like a photo. It's a stange request.
She knows we won't return to bring it back.
She stands against a tangled mass of green,
and pushes her hair back, and smooths her dress.

We're bored. We scan the faded wild life posters
for things we might have seen: deer, porcupine,
turtles, ant-eaters, toucan, and there's even
the head and shoulders portrait of a tiger.
I point out to the hills, trying to question
if there are tigers still. She shakes her head.

We drive back the way we came. The unmade track's
so clenched in trees, it lets us make-believe
in hidden tigers, yet we only see
monkeys, one lone deer, an iguana.

Then we pass huts again, and leafy clearings
of growing corn and rice. It can't be easy
surviving, when the jungle leaches back
interminably. Through flimsy walls I catch
glimpses of something shining. It seems
symbolic that each remote
man has contrived to own a looking glass.

We pass through coffee groves, then a plantation
of rubber trees, which arc into a thorax
of shadow-bars. Workers are collecting latex.
We climb down from our jeep, take photographs.

It's hard to see the edge of desecration.
Perhaps they simply pushed the boundaries back
until the seamless green was frayed and patched.
Until there was just room for one last tiger
to live without a mate, without a mirror.

Now half a world away, developed photos
release their memories. The rubber trees
look picturesque. We didn't catch the deer.
The monkeys are just dark amorphous blobs
high in the leaves, against a brilliant sky.
There's a head and shoulders portrait of the woman
using the smile she doesn't practice much.
She stands against a haze of empty green.
The sense of loneliness is deafening.

Travellers' Tales

I've travelled back from Bali, she from Kent
to share this Christmas. Sitting, drinking tea,
our conversation fluctuates between
my flight, her trip, their art, the evening's tele.
In over eighty years she hasn't travelled
further than a day trip to Dicppe.
Now, like a horror film, the world is closing
in on her. She doesn't like the dark, can't
read much now, can't manage hills regardless
of the legendary beauty of a vista. Death
is her next adventure, and she speaks
casually of it, like a planned trip.

She says she thinks she'll die before September,
since her age, eighty-one, adds up to nine,
as does next year, and also she's a three
in Numerology. That fits as well.
I say you can do anything with numbers, but she
insists, and cites as an example my sister's dying
date in sixty-six which added up to two, which was
her number. I'm glad I'm seven. I cut us some cake.
She's animated now, tallying fate to
figures. It's a customised timetable
she's guaranteed to use, eventually.

I proffer photographs. She stops politely
to look at paddies, palm trees, me in temples,
then moves unswervingly to her main question:
'Do you think that Dad and Brenda are together?
D'you think we'll all meet up in the Hereafter?'

Now in my head I visualise her walking
away, a weary figure from a station's
gloom. She's wearing her blue mac.
Outside in brilliant sunshine a group gathers,
already suntanned, dressed in summer white,
faces expectant. I have often seen
such reconciliations on my travels.

'What do you think? I'm not afraid of dying.
I'd love to meet with everyone again;
Brenda and Dad and Auntie Flo. My Joycie.'
Even this world is full of missed connections.
I can't say yes. I say it would be nice.

Dance Performance, Bali

The Gamelan strikes music, silver knives
unzip the silence. Now six gilded girls
begin the welcome dance. We watch their grace
divide time so precisely that it seems
they move in flick-card stillnesses. They turn
kaleidoscopic facets, making one
pattern. Now each faces us again.

We're seated in a vast, night-filled pavilion
amongst an audience of many nations.
We dream in other, unfamiliar landscapes.

They can't see us. They smile into the dark.

We are their silent partners. Our chairs
fan out in waves of watchfulness. Our swathe
is the wake which shadows their bright craft.
We are their leaden mirror. I have seen
this dance so many times that I could chant
its movements like a poem. Now the girls
glance over their bare shoulders, lilt their hands
coquettishly. They pick up silver bowls.
The Gamelan peals down in flickering scales.
Its music thins. The girls throw leaves and petals
as they back through the curtain into lives
like those that we'll re-enter when they've gone.
We all applaud. We softly speak in tongues
about what's next. Our laps are full of flowers.

Running

Running the spine of the hill, nothing
above me but the burst of night and the grey
and early stars, I cling to the earth's knife edge,
and the wind that loves me eddies around my rush,
and the water-mark of my flesh repeats and repeats itself
in the press of the skin-ridged air.
Time is a furrow now.
The Earth grows slow, grows slow and hums like the sea.

Yard

This
vacant cube
looks with an inward eye.
Infatuated with frugalities,
it grows beyond the lush of springing green.

This space
where sky fits neatly,
a lagoon.
Our days lie under water,
counted down,
tomorrow and tomorrow.
Now the birds
dip in and out to feed upon the corn,
dip up and down
not knowing they grow tame.

There was a boy at college,
turned insane.
Got high on acid.
thought that he could fly.
His studio was square.
So was his room.
He tried the edgelessness
of the night sky.

You've heard of time-warps?
Does this sound absurd?
It seems the granite echoes back our words,
but wearily, the walls so very old,
compressing every syllable and sigh,
each possibility, or lucky chance.
Lives merely oozing back, like stored up sun.
Tomorrow and tomorrow,
all our days.

There was a boy at college, turned insane,
He broke his back, was never quite the same.
He gave me once
a painting he had made.
It was fragmented on a jig-saw theme.
A woman in a court-yard, and the greens
were intertwined with scarlet, and with black.

This squarish space.
This cloister of no time.
It seems as if the walls project our lives.
A kind of inscape, where we chanced to fall.
Does it sound absurd to say we fly?
Dip in and out to feed upon the sky.
Dip up and down
not knowing we grow free.

The Crime

She lay, dismembered, by the high black road,
a wooden cow, drawn with a genial hand
by one familiar with the bovine race.
Then carefully cut out; a sensuous curve
described her ripening flank,
her bell-rope tail,
the yellow ochre of her valleyed back,
and jostling udder like a rubber glove.
Then neat fore-quarters, but
from fear or love,
the perpetrator had cut off her face!

He did not dump her eyes, like castor feet,
to guide the weight of flesh's furniture.
He hid her radar ears, the horny crown,
and verdant ruminations of her tongue,
her nose;
perhaps he bent, intent on art,
crafting her nostrils from grey rubberoid,
and chanced to breathe on her, so sweet, so sharp,
that from his love's infection
she caught life.

Then the board creature would have grown too wise,
and might have grassed, or been identified,
or run away, growing autonomous.

I left in mourning, slowly walking back,
walled in with stone along the dorsal track,
where armoured hawthorns rose, and crucified
themselves against the milk-white of the sky,
and gaps, like visions, sliced their vistas down
to amputated fields, slab-named with stone,
or coloured cows with calm, placated eyes.

The earth lay dormant with conspiracy,
a glut of crows rose up to net the air,
the sycamores had grown into a hook,
but nobody was speaking of the crime.

Shit Heap

With elegant precision, the steel tines
describe a scalloped rhythm. I dispatch
the air-sealed surface, crusty, odourless;
unzip the ferment of a year-deep bed,
releasing the sharp buzz of a blue stench.
The barn air steams, like
something's very hot.

The art of mucking out is to slough off
the felted straw in delicate wide sheets.
Pitchfork's a crescent moon—new-silver moon
which pares with its dipped sickle, rives and splits
slaked slumber down. Puffing, I unpack time
stored flat in formalin. The wringing stack
blooms gold and rose again, preserved in piss.
Cow-crushed and aqueous, these mermaid thins.

Each pitch lifts lightly till a certain height.
Then dead-weight focuses. I'm almost beaten
those split seconds, juggling gravity.
Then the sod's singing off.
It self-adheres across the air's brief fling
then loads and drips like so much laundry.

Absurdly heavy, when the barrow's heaped.
I push it out. Blinker my spine and eyes.
Think only in the perpendicular.
Now billow-bright, the air tries hard to trip
my wobble-wheeling, then
I'm there. I tip.

The shit-heap's not just dung. I must admit
the pleasure that its contemplation brings.
A kind of logo; folds of yellowing grass
juxtapositioning cavernous bonfire sites. Things
incompletely burnt are fluttering. Halved headlines, pictures,
even bits of verse. Or melted plastic, retching,

tight as skin.
A week ago, after two cows gave birth
I buried the placentas. Straw and dung
had gravely decomposed.
Against the earth,
a dozen cut-flower daffodils lie spent.
I tip again. The shit's an angled bank
which tenderly obscures their taffeta.

New Shoes

Half-term.
Five teenaged girls perched on the sinks
in Falmouth Public loo.
It wasn't hard
to overhear their conversation, which
was carried out in desparado shrieks.

'So then we went to Dolcis, me and Lynn.'

'And started looking round.'

'This snooty cow
came up to us, right looking down her nose,
and said, you know, "Do you need any help?"'

'We said we were just looking, but she kept
on hanging round and watching what we did
like we were shoplifters, so Tina says,
"I'm looking for some summer shoes, size five,
but not high heels, and not completely flat.
I don't mind pink or blue, or even white.
Not beige or brown." Then
ladylike we sat, but ... '

'Something set us off, I don't know what.'

'And every pair she brought out made us laugh.'

'Until the floor was littered with the stuff.'

'And Tina kept on, "Sorry that's not right."'

'And she was getting all red in the neck.'

'And we were just collapsed and couldn't stop.'

'And everyone around began to stare.'

'*And she was getting shirty, you could tell.
Then Tina says, as off-hand as you like,
"They're all old granny styles" and
I'm afraid
"I can't see anything I want today."*'

'*We laughed so much we nearly wet ourselves.
We fell about as we made for the door.*'

Two girls replied with sycophantic nods.
The fifth was a brave moralist, who said,
'*Talk about childish, if you're asking me
I think you acted rotten to the bitch!*'
But then I saw her dart a mirrored glance,
appraisingly, and smugly smile to find
a halo's not old-hat, and always fits.

Memories are Mostly Made of This

Together in the thin, brief gold of Autumn
they choose to spend this small-town Sunday walking.
There's not much open, nothing much to do.
Memories are mainly made of this.

Families and couples, thrown together
by recurrent coincidence of leisure,
seek some diversion, some shared, modest pleasure
to mark the ripples in their tides of time.

Groups split and reassemble; window shop,
or drape the safety railings by the dock,
to feed the spinning skeins of gulls with scraps
of tossed up cornet ends, and bits of bread.

Couples, sworn to long monogamy
read sex and scandal papers, side by side.
Or drink cold beer outside of colder pubs,
and watch the scudding yachts go
nowhere much.

It isn't that their love is so mundane.
There's little that's available, and cheap
enough to pass these sweet, bland hours,
won against claims of work, and chores, and sleep.
Although their highest hearts might yearn to strike
indelibly, through eroding dark,
the beacons of adventure, laughter, bliss,
often there's only this: immemorable
memories of pushing kids on bikes,
or choosing lampshades in the bargain store,
or skimming pebbles off from the grey shore
across the lilting waters. Evermore
they fly, and bounce, and sink beyond all sight,
and never go as far as one would wish,
but slowly, slowly, shape the ocean floor,
to contours huge and transient as love; and
memories are mostly made of this.

Lessons in Ecstasy

Before I learnt the nouns of passing time,
the fair's arrival simply coincided
with the horse chestnuts lighting their flower candles.
Some urban Adam, long before my birth,
had set trees single file to screen the common.
I grew within the bell-jar of their margins
of alternating sequence; pink and white.
The pink trees blossomed first: those with white candles
could be distinguished by a paler foliage,
and some had died as saplings, introducing
a notion of more enigmatic patterns.

Our council block stood square to the green space,
its brick slab face resigned. The myriad eyes
of metal windows caught the view in layers.
Sky filled the highest casements, endlessly
repeating a dull newsreel about clouds.
Our storey, three floors up, was dignified
by seeming to rest on a tree-top sea.
Our balcony curved out into the air
like a ship's rail. Even from this height,
I could only sense, rather than see
the fair's proximity; its wheels of pleasure,
which after dark, with tentacles of light,
signed deaf and dumb through bedroom curtaining,
or like a torch shone through my finger's cage,
made night reveal the colour of its blood.

And yet a fairground somehow wasn't felt
a proper interest for a girl to have.
Our rare trips kept to the periphery
amongst the penny shies and candy floss.
I did not ride sky-wheels, nor swings on chains
which pirouetted like a girl's spun skirt,
and yet such love songs trembled through the grass
even my bones rote-learnt the choruses.

Before I understood the laws of space
I'd heard a rumour that the earth was round,
so if you kept on travelling you'd get
back to the place you started. In my childhood I assumed
since nobody fell off into the sky,
and nobody could fly, except in dreams
we must live on the *inside* like a bubble.

With my eighth summer came a new attraction
which drew us; mother, sister, maiden aunt,
to take the bus two stops, beyond the place
where green perspectives narrowed out of sight.
We walked the fair's mosaic till we found
a tented cylinder, and paid to climb
up to the gallery of a great drum.

The floor was circular. A showman asked
for volunteers, and some people went down
including a young couple, she in green.

He set them with their backs against the wall,
and then the metal drum began to spin
sucking them close. Their clothes and limbs and hair
were shaped into crescent walls, like skin.
The couple started off by holding hands
but soon drifted apart. The showman made
the floor fall down and everybody clung
in random postures like a nursery frieze
in which cows can jump moons, and men called Nick
defy the gravity of candle sticks.
The audience leaned down from the curved rail
laughing and calling, but the riders spun
on silently; their faces were serene. I watched the girl.
She didn't try to keep
the mantle of her skirt below her thighs,
but closed her eyes, and spread her arms like wings.

Then the drum stopped. The riders all slid down.
And afterwards we took the long walk home
underneath trees which blotted out the sky
like a strung necklace, while the braille stars
rolled on so slowly, sometimes filtering
through fronds of palm-print leaves which foretold fortunes.
And then I knew I always had been riding,
on wheels in wheels which started in my head,
and travelled out, and on, and out of sight,
where galaxies revealed in cryptogram,
portentous mysteries of great importance
which I could not decode. Years later I'm
still trying to find words for my elation;
still wondering why funfairs make me sad.

Earth

Earth came in truck loads.
It is magic, heaped.
It is the glove of dreams
turned inside out. I would like to press
my whole flesh into it. Now in my head
I am clothed in soil.
I am earth woman, standing joyfully
above my negative, my sleeping sister, and again
and again the image repeats itself, unreeling
dark women made of earth who have lifted
themselves out of the earth, and now stare back
at their own absence. Sometimes in the line
the sisters are not earth, but are made of sky.
Then they are sky blue templates. I, earth woman, stand
speechless, immaculate, able now
to move without crumbling, and my darkness
is full of pale stones, is full of stars.

Levelling takes many days. I spread and spread the earth out
  evenly.
It becomes art, layered, meeting
an edge, a granite frame.
Now I am contained
in my domestic garden of small dreams.
The sky lids me. Light sings in rectangles.

Day after day I have trodden this earth flat,
but now I sense it changing, feel it bond
bed rock, old bones, sweet
labyrinths of dark. It is my sky arena now, my raft
of clay. It is my shadow skin
which the hills lullaby, which the fields name
as their new child. The wide earth rushes in
to claim me, comes like a mother, singing.
Sings under my stone house to gather in
the earth skin I have made. I am borne high
in its well-head of darkness, and I grasp

at bounties of night sugar. My hands press
out ghosts, the ghosts of women with clay flesh,
and each of the earth's fragments bears my thumb print.

All is silent now. The earth's curved crust
is made of women sleeping thigh to thigh.
I am the tar baby. My air claim
is a dark vacancy of dreams.
It is woman-shaped.
I am clayed in a web of names.
The sky reflects my mirror absence.

Seeing Yellow

It is a fanfare blazoned at the eye's
gate. It tastes of honey, and of brass.
Each flower is a glazed cup. Their up-shine makes
the sky reveal its canopy, as if
I'm seeing a child's drawing, with the high
blue deliniated. Hills and trees
are shaded brown and green, but only this
one patch is overlaid with wax,
with shining yellow wax, and lights a world
where everyone loves butter.

This is my image standing in the lane
between a yellow oblong set in green,
and the steep purple valley. I am sketched
as a faint pencil ghost, but coloured in
with the same yellow wax, as if I'm lit
from inside, like a candle in a clay
cauldron. I might break
from so much yellow heat. Now I've walked on
and must be drawn again.

Now yellow is a single angel's wing
which flies behind my head. The sky's balloon
has burst, and troupes of yellow-bellied clouds
slither and grin through air's uncharted ocean.

Author's note

I was born in Peckham Rye, London in 1944. My father lost his sight in an accident shortly after my birth, and the family lived thereafter in fairly frugal style in council-house accommodation. Throughout my childhood I acted as my father's 'eyes', describing things to him, helping with gardening and carpentry, reading to him and guiding his excursions. We even learnt braille together! I feel that these early experiences have had a lasting effect on the character of my own perceptions.

In 1961 I became a student at Goldsmiths' College, London University, where I studied painting, obtaining a B.A. degree in fine art in 1965. While at Goldsmiths' I met and married a fellow student, and gave birth to the first two of our three children. After leaving college I held two one-man exhibitions of my paintings, and also had work in group shows in London and Paris.

Like many art graduates, my idealistic ambition was to earn my living as a painter. However, two or three years and a third child later, our need for a stable income became extreme, and almost accidently I began a teaching career which was to last for twelve years. After a stint in Primary education I took an appointment teaching emotionally disturbed adolescents (at the school upon which the film 'The Making of Miss McMichael', starring Oliver Reed and Judi Dench, was based). Later I taught for three years in a unit for younger dyslexic children. During this period my memories are of rather frantic overwork. Painting became too impractical to include in a routine which contained three small children and a full-time job. However I had always written since childhood, and particularly poetry, and this grew from a peripheral activity into my creative mainstay. I didn't seek to publish the writing produced at this time, and in fact systematically threw it away!

Nine years ago my husband Fred and I decided to seek a 'life change' situation which would provide a quieter and more aesthetic environment, and also time to pursue our personal interests. This resulted in a move to Cornwall, where we live on an eleven acre smallholding which I run as a beef and dairy enterprise.

Fred and I have always shared a desire to travel, and early last year, after our first holiday to the Far East, we decided to try to finance this ambition by bringing back a small number of art and craft objects for resale in the U.K. We began very modestly, with sales made through small Art Galleries, and in our marvellous local village shop, where to this day flying dragons are suspended over the sliced bread, and in the window tiger and demon masks lean nonchalantly against tins of syrup. The enterprise has grown, and recently we opened our own gallery in Falmouth. We now make four or five buying trips a year to Bali, Indonesia, and next year plan to extend our travels to Thailand, and then perhaps South America.

My first response to Bali was a kind of voyeurism; the new sights and sounds were observed and enjoyed but not assimilated into any kind of 'internal landscape', and it was some months before references to them appeared in my poetry. However I am finding that familiarity with this second culture can serve to clarify existing, analogous ideas. In the West the metaphysical side of man's nature is often devalued and made unconscious. In Bali, where religion and the performing arts combine to express themselves through ritual and the re-enactment of myths, then archetypal images are made conscious, and can be recognised for what they are. Travel also serves to shock the senses alive, so that on my return even the beautiful and austere Cornish landscape is seen with fresh eyes.

One of the great bonuses of giving up a time-tabled job has been the deregulation of time. This does not mean that time is unstructured; indeed living and working in a rural environment has increased my awareness of the interplay of energies and rhythms that surround and influence us all; and not only our physical bodies, but our behaviour patterns, our thoughts and dreams. It would seem that much which appears visionary or inspirational in both art and science is, in fact, an act of recognition of these commonly felt but largely unacknowledged influences.

Many of my poems have developed from this fascination with the complexities of time; the ongoing relationship between several diverse but parallel experiences. Perhaps my training as an artist has encouraged me to retain impressions visually, and to seek visual models for abstract ideas. Sometimes I 'freeze-frame' experiences into a series of visual tableaux, and from these write poems consisting of several chronological stanzas, as in 'Seeing Yellow', 'Earth', 'Pendulums' and 'Dance Performance, Bali'.

In our society involvement in the arts is often considered to be an élitist or eccentric activity. We regard culture much as we regard the forces of Nature; while we pay lip service to the aesthetic qualities of both, we regard their nurture as an optional extra, and one which is financially unviable. Yet I am becoming increasingly convinced that man's salvation lies in his instinct towards personal creativity; for it is through the processes of creative thought that we are able to form coherent links between memory, imagination, discovery and experience. We are regenerated by our association with the arts, which serve to link us with the mystical and spiritual aspects of our own experience. Through the process of creativity language is renewed and finds definition.

Maureen Wilkinson